Stories of Boys and Girls Who Loved the Saviour

James Janeway

Alpha Editions

This edition published in 2024

ISBN : 9789362921147

Design and Setting By
Alpha Editions
www.alphaedis.com
Email - info@alphaedis.com

Contents

LITTLE SARAH HOWLEY.

MISS SARAH HOWLEY, when she was between eight and nine years old, was carried by her friends to hear a sermon, where the minister preached upon Matt. xi, 30, "My yoke is easy, and my burden is light;" in the applying of which scripture the child was mightily awakened, and made deeply sensible of the condition of her soul, and her need of Christ: she wept bitterly to think what a case she was in; went home, retired into a chamber, and upon her knees she wept and cried to the Lord as well as she could, which might easily be perceived by her eyes and countenance.

2. She was not contented with this, but got her little brother and sister into a chamber with her, and told them their condition by nature, and wept over them, and prayed with them.

3. After this, she heard another sermon upon Prov. xxix, 15 "He that, being often reproved, hardeneth his neck, shall suddenly be destroyed, and that without remedy;" at which she was more affected than before, and was so exceedingly solicitous about her soul, that she spent great part of the night in weeping and praying, and could scarcely take any rest, day nor night, for some time together; desiring with all her soul to escape from everlasting flames, and to get an interest in the Lord Jesus: O what should she do for Christ! what should she do to be saved!

4. She gave herself much to attending upon the word preached, and still continued very tender under it, greatly relishing what she heard.

5. She was very much in secret prayer, and was usually very importunate, and full of tears.

6. She could scarcely speak of sin, or be spoken to, but her heart was ready to melt.

7. She spent much time in reading the Scripture.

8. She was exceedingly dutiful to her parents, very loath to grieve them in the least: and if she had at any time (which was very rare) offended them, she would weep bitterly.

9. She abhorred lying, and allowed herself in no known sin.

10. When she was at school, she was eminent for her diligence, teachableness, meekness, and modesty, speaking little, but when she did speak, it was usually spiritual.

11. She continued in this course of religious duties for some years together.

12. When she was about fourteen years old, she broke a vein in her lungs, (as is supposed,) and often spat blood, yet did a little recover.

13. In the beginning of January, she was taken very bad again, in which sickness she was in great distress of soul. When she was first taken, she said, "O mother, pray for me, for Satan is so busy that I cannot pray for myself; I see I am undone without Christ, and a pardon! O, I am undone to all eternity!"

14. Her mother, knowing how serious she had been formerly, did a little wonder that she should be in such agonies; and asked her what sin it was that was so burdensome to her spirit? "O mother," said she, "it is not any particular sin that sticks so close to my conscience, as the sin of my nature: without the blood of Christ that will damn me."

15. Her mother asked her what she should pray for, for her? She answered, "That I may have a saving knowledge of Jesus Christ; and that I may have an assurance of God's love to my soul." Her mother asked her why she spoke so little to the minister that came to her? She answered, "It was her duty with patience and silence to learn of him."

16. One time when she fell into a fit, she cried out, "O I am going; I am going: but what shall I do to be saved? Lord Jesus, I will lie at thy feet; and if I perish, it shall be at the fountain of thy mercy."

17. She was much afraid of presumption, and dreaded a mistake in the matters of her soul, and would be often putting up ejaculations to God, to deliver her from deceiving herself. To instance in one, "Great and mighty God," said she, "let my faith be a true faith; that I may not be a foolish virgin, having a lamp, but no oil."

18. Her father bade her be of good cheer, because she was going to a better Father; at which she fell into a great agony, and said, "But how do I know that? I am a poor sinner, who wants assurance; O for assurance!"

This was her great, earnest, and constant request to all who came to her, to beg assurance for her; and she would look with so much eagerness upon them, as if she desired nothing in the world so much as that they would pity her, and help her with their prayers. Never was a poor creature more earnest for any thing than she was for assurance and the light of God's countenance. O the piteous moan that she would make! O the agony that her soul was in!

19. The Lord's day before that on which she died, a kinsman of hers came to see her, and asked her whether she knew him? She answered, "Yes, I know you, and I desire you would learn to know Christ. You are young, but you know not how soon you may die! and, O, to die without Christ is a

fearful thing! O, redeem time! O, time, time, precious time!" Being requested by him not to spend herself, she said, "She would fain do all the good she could while she lived;" upon which account she desired that a sermon might be preached at her funeral, concerning the preciousness of time.

20. Some ministers who came to see her earnestly entreated the Lord to give her some token for good, that she might die in full triumph: notes of the same nature were sent to several churches.

21. After she had long waited for an answer to their prayers, she said, "Well, I will venture my soul upon Christ."

22. Considering the pains and agonies that she was in, her patience was next to a wonder: "Lord," said she, "Lord, give me patience, that I may not dishonour thee!"

23. On Thursday, after long waiting, great fears, and many prayers, when all her friends thought she had been past speaking, to the astonishment of her friends, she broke forth thus, with a very audible voice, and cheerful countenance: "Lord, thou hast promised that whosoever come unto thee thou wilt in no wise cast them out: Lord, I come unto thee, and surely thou wilt in no wise cast me out; O, so precious! O, so glorious is Jesus! I have thee! Blessed and glorious is Jesus; he is precious, he is precious! O, the admirable love of God in sending Christ and free grace to a poor lost creature!"

24. Her soul then seemed ravished with the love of Christ. And while she was engaged in magnifying of God, her father, brothers, and sisters, with others of the family, were called, to whom she spake particularly as her strength would give leave. She gave her Bible as a legacy to one of her brothers, and desired him to use that well for her sake; and added, to him and the rest, "O make use of time to get Christ for your souls: spend no time in running up and down, or in playing: O get Christ for your souls while you are young! Remember now your Creator before you come to a sick bed: put not off this great work till then, for then you will find it hard work indeed: I know by experience the devil will tell you it is time enough; and you are young, and what need you be in such haste? you will have time enough when you are old. But remember the words of a dying sister. If you knew how good Christ is! if you had but one taste of his sweetness, you had rather go to him a thousand times than stay in this wicked world. I would not for ten thousand worlds part with my interest in Christ. O, how happy am I that I am going to everlasting joys! I would not go back again for twenty thousand worlds; and will you not strive to get an interest in Christ?"

25. After this, looking upon one of her father's servants, she said, "What shall I do at the great day, when Christ shall say to me, 'Come, thou blessed of my Father, inherit the kingdom prepared for thee?' and shall say to the wicked, 'Go, thou cursed, into the lake that burns for ever!' What a grief is it for me to think that I should see any of my friends that I knew upon earth, turned into that lake which burns for ever! O that word, for ever! Remember that for ever! I speak these words to you, but they are nothing except God speaks to you too: O pray that God would give you grace!" And then she prayed, "O Lord, finish thy work upon their souls: it will be my comfort to see you in glory; but it will be your everlasting happiness."

26. On Friday, after she had had such lively discoveries of God's love, she was exceedingly desirous to die, and cried out, "Come, Lord Jesus, come quickly! Conduct me to thy tabernacle. I am a poor creature without thee; but, Lord Jesus, my soul longs to be with thee: O when shall it be? Why not now, blessed Jesus? Come, Lord Jesus, come quickly! But why do I thus speak? Thy time, my Lord, is the best: O, give me patience."

27. On Saturday she spoke but little, being very drowsy, yet now and then she dropped these words, "How long, O blessed Jesus? Finish thy work, holy Jesus: come away, Lord Jesus, come quickly!"

28. On the Lord's day she scarcely spoke any thing. She requested that notes of thanksgiving might be sent to those who had formerly prayed for her, that they might help her to praise the Lord for that full assurance which he had given her of his love; and seemed to be swallowed up with the thoughts of God's free love to her soul. She often commended her spirit into the hand of the Lord. The last words she was heard to utter were these, "Lord, help, Lord Jesus, help! my Lord Jesus, blessed Jesus!" Thus on the Lord's day, between nine and ten o'clock in the evening, she sweetly slept in Jesus, and began an everlasting Sabbath, February 19, 1670.

A HAPPY BOY.

A LITTLE CHILD whose mother had dedicated him to the Lord in infancy, when he could not speak plain would be crying after God, and was greatly desirous to be taught good things.

2. He could not endure to be put to bed without prayer, but would put his parents upon it, with much devotion kneel down, and with great patience and delight continue till it was concluded, without the least sign of being weary. He seemed never so well pleased as when so engaged.

3. He could not be satisfied with family prayer, but he would often be upon his knees by himself in one corner or another.

4. He was much delighted in hearing the word of God either read or preached.

5. He loved to go to school, that he might learn something of God, and would take great notice of what he had read, and come home and speak of it with much affection. He would rejoice in his book, and say to his mother, "O mother, I had a sweet lesson to-day: will you please to give me leave to fetch my book, that you may hear it?"

6. He quickly learned to read the Scripture, and would, with great reverence, tenderness, and groans, read till tears and sobs were ready to hinder him.

7. When he was at secret prayer he would weep bitterly.

8. He was wont often to complain of the wickedness of his heart, and seemed to be more grieved for the corruption of his nature, than, for actual sin.

9. He was much troubled for the wandering of his thoughts in prayer, and that he could not always keep his heart fixed upon God, and his affections more constantly raised.

10. He kept a watch over his heart, and observed the workings of his soul, and would complain that they were so vain and foolish, and so little busied about spiritual things.

11. He was exceedingly importunate with God in prayer, and would plead with God at an unusual rate; and he would beg and expostulate, and weep so, that sometimes it could not be kept from the ears of the neighbours: so that one in the next house was forced to cry out, "The prayers and tears of that child in the next house will sink me to hell!" because by it he did condemn his neglect of prayer and his slight performance of it.

12. He abhorred lying with all his soul.

13. When he had committed any sin, he was easily convinced of it, and would get into some corner, or secret place, and with tears beg pardon of God, and strength to guard against it.

14. When other children were at play, he would be praying.

15. A friend of his asked him, when he was first taken sick, whether he was not willing to die? He answered, No! because he was afraid of his state as to another world. "Why, child," said the other, "thou didst pray for a new heart, for an humble and sincere heart, and I have heard thee: didst thou not pray with thy heart?" "I hope I did," rejoined he.

16. Not long after, the same person asked him again, "If he was willing to die?" He answered, "Now I am willing, for I shall go to Christ."

17. He still grew weaker and weaker, but behaved with a great deal of sweetness and patience, waiting for his change. At last, calling upon the name of the Lord, and saying, "Lord Jesus, Lord Jesus!" he sweetly slept, dying when he was between five and six years old.

HAPPY MARY.

MARY A., when she was between four and five years old, was greatly affected in hearing the word of God, and became very solicitous about her soul, weeping bitterly to think what would become of her in another world, asking strange questions concerning God, and Christ, and her own soul. So that before she was full five years old, she minded the one thing needful, and chose the better part.

2. She was wont to be much in secret prayer, and many times came from her knees with tears.

3. She would choose such times and places for secret prayer as might render her less observed by others: and endeavoured to conceal what she was doing when she was engaged therein.

4. Her mother being full of sorrow after the death of her husband, this child came to her and asked her why she wept so exceedingly? Her mother answered that she had cause enough to weep, because her father was dead. "No, dear mother," said the child, "you have no cause to weep so much, for God is a good God still."

5. She was a dear lover of faithful ministers. One time after she had been hearing Mr. Whitaker, she said, "I love that man dearly for the sweet words he speaks concerning Christ."6. Her book was her delight; and many times she was so strangely affected in reading the Scriptures, that she burst out into tears, and would hardly be pacified: so greatly was she taken with Christ's sufferings, the zeal of God's servants, and the danger of a natural state.7. She often complained of the corruption of her nature, of the hardness of her heart, that she could repent no more, and be no more humble and grieved for her sins against a good God; and when she thus complained, it was with abundance of tears.8. She was very conscientious in keeping the Sabbath, spending the whole time in reading or praying, learning her catechism, or teaching her brothers and sisters. One time when she was left at home on the Lord's day, she got some other little children together, with her brothers and sisters, and told them that it was the Lord's day, and they ought to remember it to keep it holy. She then told them it was to be spent in religious exercises all the day, except so much as was taken up in the works of necessity and mercy: then she prayed with them, and among other things begged that the Lord would give grace and wisdom to them, (little children,) that they might know how to serve him.

9. At another time a near relation of hers being in some straits, made some complaint, to whom she said, "I have heard Mr. Garter say, 'A man may go to heaven without a penny in his purse, but not without grace in his heart.'"

10. She had an extraordinary love to the people of God: and when she saw any who she thought feared the Lord, her heart would even leap for joy.

11. When she was between eleven and twelve years old, she sickened of the plague, in which she behaved with admirable patience and sweetness, and did what she could with Scripture arguments to support and encourage her relations to part with her, who was going to glory, and to prepare themselves to meet her in a blessed eternity.

12. She was not many days sick before she was marked with the complaint which she first saw herself, and was greatly rejoiced to think that she was marked out for the Lord, and was now going apace to Christ. She called to her friends and said, "I am marked, but be not troubled, for I know I am marked for one of the Lord's own." One asked her how she knew that? She answered, "The Lord hath told me that I am one of his dear children." And this she spoke with a holy confidence in the Lord's love, and was not in the least daunted at the approach of death; but seemed greatly delighted in the apprehension of her nearness to her Father's house. And it was not long before she was filled with joy unspeakable in believing.

13. When she lay dying, her mother came to her, and told her she was sorry she had so frequently reproved and corrected so good a child; "O mother," said she, "speak not thus: I bless God, now I am dying, for your reproofs and corrections too: for, it may be, I might have gone to hell, if it had not been for your reproofs and corrections."14. Some of the neighbours came to visit her, and asked her if she could leave them. She answered, "If you serve the Lord, you will come after me to glory."15. A little before she died, she had a great conflict with Satan, and cried out, "I am none of his." Her mother seeing her troubled, asked her what was the matter? She answered, "Satan did trouble me, but now, I thank God, all is well. I know I am none of his, but Christ's."

16. After this she had a great sense of God's love, and a glorious sight, as if she had seen the very heavens open, and the angels coming to receive her; by which her heart was filled with joy, and her tongue with praise.

17. Being desired by the bystanders to give them a particular account of what she saw, she answered, "You shall know hereafter:" and so in an ecstasy of joy and triumph, she went to God when she was about twelve years old.

PRAYING CHARLIE.

CHARLES BRIDGEMAN had no sooner learned to speak, but he betook himself to prayer.

2. He was very prone to learn the things of God.

3. He would be sometimes teaching those persons that waited upon him their duty.

4. He learned by heart many good things before he was well fit to go to school. And when he was sent to school, he carried it so that all that observed him, either did or might admire him. O, the sweet temper, the good disposition, the sincere religion which was in the child!

5. When he was at school what was it that he desired to learn but Christ and him crucified?

6. So religious and savoury were his words, his actions so upright, his devotions so hearty, his fear of God so great, that many were ready to say as they did of John,—What manner of child shall this be?

7. He would be much in reading the Holy, Scriptures.

8. He was desirous of more spiritual knowledge, and would be oft asking very serious and admirable questions.

9. He would not stir out of doors before he had poured out his soul to the Lord in prayer.10. When he ate any thing, he would be sure to lift up his heart unto the Lord for a blessing upon it; and when he had moderately refreshed himself by eating, he would not forget to acknowledge God's goodness in feeding him.11. He would not lie down in his bed till he had been upon his knees; and when sometimes he had forgotten his duty, he would quickly get out of his bed, and kneeling down upon his bare knees, ask God's forgiveness of that sin.12. He would rebuke his brethren, if they were at any time too hasty at their meals, and did eat without asking a blessing; his check was this: "Dare you do thus? God be merciful to us! this bit of bread might choke us."

13. His sentences were wise and weighty, and might well become some ancient Christian.

14. His sickness was a lingering disease: against which, to comfort him, one tells him of possessions that must fall to his portion; "And what are they?" said he, "I had rather have the kingdom of heaven than a thousand such inheritances."

15. When he was sick he seemed much taken up with heaven, and asked very serious questions about the nature of the soul.

16. After he was pretty well satisfied about that, he inquired how his soul might be saved? The answer being made, "By the applying of Christ's merit by faith:" he was pleased with the answer, and was ready to give any one that should desire it an account of his hope.

17. Being asked whether he had rather live or die? he answered, "I desire to die, that I may go to my Saviour."

18. His pains increasing upon him, one asked him whether he would rather still endure those pains or forsake Christ? "Alas!" said he, "I know not what to say, being a child: for these pains may stagger a strong man; but I will strive to endure the best I can." Upon this he called to mind that martyr, *Thomas Bilney*, who, being in prison the night before his burning, put his finger into the candle to know how he could endure the fire; "O," said the child, "had I lived then, I would have run through the fire to have gone to Christ."

19. His sickness lasted long: and at least three days before his death he prophesied his departure, and not only that he must die, but the very day. "On the Lord's day," said he, "look to me;" neither was this a word of course, which you may guess by his frequent repetition, every day asking till the day came indeed, "What, is Sunday come?" At last, the looked-for day came on; and no sooner had the sun beautified that morning with its light, but he falls into a trance, his eyes were fixed, his face cheerful, his lips smiling, his hands and arms clasped in a bow, as if he would have embraced some blessed angel that was at hand to receive his soul. But he comes to himself, and tells them how he saw the sweetest body that ever eyes beheld, who bid him to be of good cheer, for he must presently go with him.

20. One that stood near him, as now suspecting the time of his dissolution nigh, bid him say, "Lord, into thy hands I commend my spirit, which is thy due; for why? thou hast redeemed it, O Lord, my God, most true!"

21. The last words which he spoke were exactly these: "Pray, pray, pray, nay, yet pray, and the more prayers the better all prospers; God is the best physician; into thy hands I commend my spirit. O Lord Jesus receive my soul: now close mine eyes: forgive me, father, mother, brother, sister, all the world. Now I am well; my pain is almost gone, my joy is at hand. Lord, have mercy on me. O Lord, receive my soul unto thee." And thus he yielded up his spirit unto the Lord when he was about twelve years old.

A POOR BUT HAPPY BOY.

A VERY poor child, of the parish of Newington-Butts, came to the door of a friend of mine, in a very lamentable case: it pleased God to raise in the heart of my friend a great pity and tenderness toward him: so that he took him out of the streets, who had nothing at all to commend him to any one's charity but his misery. My friend, seeking the glory of God, discharged the parish of the child, and took him as his own; yet there seemed to be little hopes of doing good upon him, for he was a very monster of wickedness, and a thousand times more miserable and vile by his sin than by his poverty. He was running to hell as fast as he could go, and was old in vice when he was but young in years: we scarcely hear of one so like the devil in his infancy as was this poor child. What sin was there that his age was capable of, which he did not commit? What by the corruption of his nature, and the abominable example of little beggar boys, he was indeed arrived at a great pitch of impiety. He would call names, take God's name in vain, curse, swear, and do all kinds of mischief; and as to any thing of God, he was worse than a heathen.

2. No sooner had this good man taken this creature into his house but he prayed for him, and laboured with all his might to convince him of his miserable condition by nature, and to teach him something of God, the worth of his own soul, and that eternity of glory or misery to which he was bound. And, blessed be God, it was not long before the Lord was pleased to let him understand that it was himself who put into his heart to take in this child. The Lord soon blessed his instructions, so that an amazing change was seen. In the space of a few weeks he was convinced of the evil of his ways; no more calling of names, swearing or cursing, no more taking of the Lord's name in vain. His company, his talk, his employment, were changed, and he was like another creature.

3. And this change was not only an external one, but he would get by himself, and weep and mourn bitterly for his wicked life.

4. He was still more and more broken under a sense of his undone state by nature; often in tears, and bemoaning his lost and miserable condition. When his master spoke of the things of God, he listened earnestly, and took in with much eagerness and affection, what he was taught. There was seldom any discourse about religion in his hearing, but he heard as though it were for his life.

5. Thus he continued seeking after the knowledge of God, till the sickness came into the house, with which he was smitten. At his first sickening the

poor child was greatly amazed and afraid; and though his pains were great, and the distemper very tedious; nevertheless, the sense of his sins, and the thought of the condition that his soul was still in, made his trouble ten times greater.

6. He was in grievous agonies of spirit; his former sins stared him in the face, and made him tremble. The poison of God's arrows did even drink up his spirits; the sense of sin and of wrath were so great that he knew not what to do. The weight of God's displeasure, and the thought of lying under it to all eternity, broke him even to pieces, and he bitterly cried out, "What shall I do! I am a miserable sinner, and I fear that I shall go to hell." His sins had been so great and so many, that there was no hope for him. He was not by far so much concerned for his life as for his soul: what would become of that for ever. Now the plague upon his body seemed nothing to that which was in his soul.

7. He not only cried out against his swearing, lying, and other outward notorious sins; but was in great horror for the sin of his nature; the vileness and original corruption of his heart. For this he was in so great anguish that the trouble of his spirit made him forget the pain of his body.

8. He very particularly confessed and bewailed his sins, and some sins so secret that none in the world could charge him with.

9. He would ask others whether they thought there were any hopes for him, and would beg of them to deal plainly with him; for he was greatly afraid of being deceived.

10. Being informed how willing and ready the Lord Jesus Christ was to accept of poor sinners, and being counselled to venture himself upon Christ for mercy and salvation, he said he would fain cast himself upon Christ, but he could not but wonder how Christ should die for such a vile wretch as he was, and he found it one of the hardest things in the world to believe.

11. But at last it pleased the Lord to give him some hope that there might be mercy for him, the chief of sinners; and he was enabled to lay hold upon that, "Come unto me all ye that are weary and heavy laden, and I will give you rest." Nor was it long before he was full of praise and admiration of God; so that, to speak in the words of one that was an eye and ear witness, he was so full of joy and praise that he longed for heaven.

12. He now grew exceedingly in knowledge, experience, patience, humility, and self-abhorrence. He prayed before, but now the Lord poured out upon him the spirit of prayer in an extraordinary manner; so that now he prayed more frequently, more earnestly, more spiritually than ever. O how eagerly would he beg to be washed in the blood of Jesus! And that the King of

kings, and Lord of lords, who was over heaven and earth, would pardon and forgive him all his sins, and receive his soul into his kingdom. And what he spoke was with so much life and fervour of spirit, that it filled the hearers with astonishment and joy.

13. He had no small sense of the use and excellence of Christ, and such longings and breathings of his soul after him, that when mention has been made of Christ, he hath been ready to leap out of his bed for joy.

14. The Wednesday before he died, he lay in a trance for about half an hour, in which time he thought he saw a vision of angels. When he was out of his trance, he asked his nurse why she did not let him go? "Go! whither?" said she; "Why, along with those lovely gentlemen," said he; "but they told me they would come and fetch me away upon Friday." And he repeated these words many times, "Upon Friday next those lovely gentlemen will come for me."

15. He was very thankful to his master, and very sensible of his great kindness in taking him out of the streets when begging, and he admired the goodness of God, which put it into the mind of a stranger: said he, "I hope to see you in heaven, for I am sure you will go thither. O blessed, blessed be God, that made you to take pity upon me; for I might have died, and have gone to the devil, and been damned for ever, if it had not been for you."

16. The Thursday before he died, he asked a friend of mine what he thought of his condition, and whither his soul was going? for he said he could not still but fear, lest he should deceive himself with false hopes. At which my friend spoke to him thus:—"If thou art but willing to accept of Christ, thou mayest have Christ, and all that thou dost want with him. Thou sayest thou fearest that Christ will not accept of thee! I fear that thou art not heartily willing to accept of him." The child answered, "Indeed I am." "Why, then, if thou art unfeignedly willing to have Christ, I tell thee he is a thousand times more willing to have thee, and wash thee, and save thee. And now at this time, Christ offers himself to thee again; therefore, receive him humbly by faith into thy heart, and bid him welcome, for he deserveth it." Upon which words the Lord discovered his love to the child; and he gave a kind of leap in his bed, and snapped his finger and thumb together with abundance of joy. And from that time forward, in full joy and assurance of God's love, he continued earnestly praising God, desiring to die, and to be with Christ. And on Friday morning he sweetly went to rest, using that expression, "Into thy hands, O Lord, I commit my spirit!" being not much above nine years old.

A BABE IN CHRIST.

JOHN SUDLOW was born of religious parents, in the county of Middlesex, whose care was to instill spiritual principles into him as soon as he was capable of understanding them, whose endeavours the Lord was pleased to crown with the desired success.

2. When he was scarce able to speak plain he seemed to have a very great awe and reverence of God upon his spirit, and a strange sense of the things of another world.

3. The first thing that much affected him, and made him endeavour to escape from the wrath to come, and to inquire what he should do to be saved, was the death of a little brother. When he saw him without breath, and not able to speak or stir; and when carried out of doors, and put into the ground, he was greatly concerned, and asked whether he should die too? Being answered yes it made so deep an impression on him, that from that time forward, he was exceedingly serious; and this was when he was about four years old.

4. He was now desirous to know what he might do that he might live in another world, and what to avoid, that he might not die for ever. And, being instructed by his parents, he soon laboured to avoid whatsoever might displease God. Now the apprehensions of God, death and eternity, laid such a restraint upon him, that he would not, for a world, have told a lie. He was much taken with reading the book of martyrs, and would willingly leave his dinner and go to his book.

5. He went to his father and mother with great tenderness and compassion, and entreated them to take more care of his brothers and sisters; and to take heed lest they should go to hell, and be ruined for ever.

6. The providences of God were not passed by without his minute observation. In the time of the plague he was exceedingly concerned about his everlasting state, and was very much by himself upon his knees. The following prayer was found written in short hand after his death.

7. O Lord God and merciful Father, take pity upon me, a miserable sinner: and strengthen me, O Lord, in thy faith, and make me one of thy saints in heaven. O Lord, keep me from this poisonous infection; however, not my will, but thy will be done. O Lord, if thou hast appointed me to die by it, fit me for death, and give me a good heart to bear up under my afflictions. O Lord God, and merciful Father, take pity on me, thy child. Teach me, O Lord, thy word; make me strong in faith. O Lord, I have sinned against

thee; Lord, pardon my sins. I had been in hell long ago if it had not been for thy mercy. But, O Lord, if thou hast appointed me to die, fit me for death, that I may die with comfort. And, O Lord, I pray thee to help me to bear up under my afflictions for Christ's sake. Amen.

8. He was not a little concerned for the whole nation, and begged that God would pardon the sins of this land, and bring it nearer to himself.

9. About the beginning of November, this child was smote with the distemper, but he behaved with admirable patience under the hand of God.

10. These were some of his last expressions. "The Lord shall be my physician, for he will cure both soul and body. Heaven is the best hospital. It is the Lord, let him do what seemeth good in his eyes." Again, "It is the Lord that taketh away my health; but I will say as Job did, 'Blessed be the name of the Lord.' If I should live longer, I should but sin against God." Looking upon his father, he said, "If the Lord will but lend me the least finger of his hand to lead me through the dark entry of death, I will rejoice in him."

11. When a minister came to him, among other things, he spake something of life. He answered, "This is a wicked world: it is better to live in heaven."

12. An hour and a half before his death, the same minister came again to visit him, and asked him, "John, art thou not afraid to die?" He answered, "No, if the Lord will comfort me in that hour." "But," said the minister, "how canst thou expect comfort, seeing we deserve none?" He answered, "No, if I had my deserts, I had been in hell long ago." "But," replied the minister, "which way dost thou expect comfort and salvation, seeing that thou art a sinner?" He answered, "In Christ alone." In whom, about an hour and a half after, he fell asleep.

THE MINISTER'S DAUGHTER.

TABITHA ALDER was the daughter of a minister in Kent, who lived near Gravesend. She was instructed in the Holy Scriptures by her father and mother; but there appeared nothing extraordinary in her till she was between seven and eight years old:

2. About which time, when she was sick, one asked her what she thought would become of her if she should die? She answered that she was greatly afraid she should go to hell.

3. Being asked why she was afraid she should go to hell? She answered, because she did not love God.

4. Again, being asked how she knew that she did not love God? she replied, "What have I done for God ever since I was born? And beside this, I have been taught that he that loves God keeps his commandments; but I have kept none of them."

5. Being farther demanded if she would not fain love God? she answered, "Yes, with all my heart, if I could, but I find it a hard thing to love one I do not see."

6. She was advised to beg of God a heart to love him: she answered, "I am afraid it is too late."

7. Upon this, seeing her in such a desponding condition, a friend of hers spent the next day in fasting and prayer for her.

8. After this, that friend asked her how she did now? She answered with a great deal of joy, "Now I bless the Lord; I love the Lord Jesus dearly; I feel I do love him. O, I love him dearly."

9. "Why," said her friend, "did you not say yesterday you did not love the Lord, and that you could not?" "Sure," said she, "it was Satan hindered me. But now I love him. O blessed be God for the Lord Jesus Christ."

10. After this she had a discovery of her approaching dissolution, which was no small comfort to her: "Anon," said she, (with a holy triumph,) "I shall be with Jesus. I am married to him: he is my husband: I am his bride: I have given myself to him, and he hath given himself to me, and I shall live with him for ever."

11. This language struck the hearers with astonishment. She still continued in a kind of ecstasy of joy, admiring the excellence of Christ, rejoicing in her interest in him, and longing to be with him.

12. After a while, some of her friends, who stood near her, observed a more than ordinary earnestness and fixedness in her countenance; they said one to another, "Look how earnestly she looks, surely she sees something."

13. One asked her what it was that she fixed her eyes upon so eagerly? "I warrant," says one, "she saw death coming."

14. "No," said she, "it is the glory that I saw, it is that on which my eyes were fixed."

15. One demanded of her, what the glory was like? She replied, "I cannot tell what, but I am going to it: will you go with me? I am going to glory. O that you were all going with me to that glory!" With these words her soul took wings, and went to the possession of that glory. She died when she was between eight and nine years of age.

LITTLE JACOB'S FAITH.

JACOB BICKS was born in Leyden, in the year 1657. He was visited with sickness upon the 6th of August, 1664. In his distemper he was very sleepy till near his death, but when he did awake he was wont still to fall a praying.

2. Once when his parents had prayed with him, they asked him if they should once more send for the physician? "No," said he, "I will have the doctor no more; the Lord will help me; I know he will take me to himself."

3. When his parents had prayed with him, he said, "Come, now, dear father and mother, and kiss me: I know that I shall die. Farewell, dear father and mother; farewell, dear sister; farewell, all. Now shall I go unto God and Jesus Christ, and the holy angels. Father, know you not what is said by Jeremiah? 'Blessed is he who trusteth in the Lord.' Now I trust in him, and he will bless me; and in 1 John ii, it is said, 'Little children, love not the world, for the world passeth away.'"

4. "Away then all that is in the world, away with all my pleasant things in the world; away with my dagger, for where I go there is nothing to do with daggers and swords; men shall not fight there, but praise God. Away with all my books: there shall I learn true wisdom without books."

5. His father said, "My dear child, the Lord will be near thee, and uphold thee."

6. "Yea, father," said he, "the Apostle Peter saith, 'God resisteth the proud, but he giveth grace to the humble.' I humble myself under the mighty hand of God, and he shall help me and lift me up."

7. "O, my dear child," said his father, "hast thou so strong faith?"

8. "Yes," said he, "God hath given me so strong a faith in himself through Jesus Christ, that the devil shall flee from me: for it is said, He who believeth in the Son hath everlasting life, and he hath overcome the wicked one. Now I believe in Jesus Christ my Redeemer, and he will not leave nor forsake me, but shall give unto me eternal life, and then I shall sing, Holy, holy, holy, is the Lord of Sabaoth."

Then, with that word, "Lord, be merciful unto me a poor sinner," he quietly breathed out his soul, being about seven years old.

JACOB'S SISTER SUSANNAH.

SUSANNAH BICKS, the sister of Jacob Bicks, was born in Leyden, in Holland, January 24, 1650, of religious parents, whose great care was to instruct their child, and to present her to the ministers of the place to be publicly instructed.

2. It pleased God to bless this to her soul, so that she had soon a true relish for what she was taught, and made an admirable use of it in time of need.

3. She was a child of great dutifulness to her parents, and of a very sweet, humble nature; and not only the truth, but the power and eminence of religion did shine in her.

4. In August, 1664, when the pestilence raged in Holland, as she felt herself very ill, she broke forth in these words, "If thy law were not my delight, I should perish in my affliction."

5. Her father coming to her, said, "Be of good comfort, my child, for the Lord will be near to thee and us: he will not forsake us, though he chastens." "Yea, father," said she, "our heavenly Father doth chasten us for our profit, that we may be partakers of his holiness; no chastisement seemeth for the present to be joyous, but grievous; but afterward it yields the peaceable fruits of righteousness to them which are exercised thereby."

6. After this, with her eyes lifted towards heaven, she said, "Be merciful to me a sinner, according to thy word."

7. She greatly abhorred sin, and, with much grief and self-detestation, reflected upon it; but that which lay the closest to her heart was the depravity of her nature. She often cried out in the words of the psalmist, "Behold, I was shapen in iniquity, and in sin did my mother conceive me." She could never lay herself low enough under a sense of that sin which she brought with her into the world.

8. That scripture dwelt much on her tongue, "The sacrifices of God are a broken heart; a broken and contrite spirit, O God, thou wilt not despise." "O for that brokenness of heart," said she, "which flows from faith, and for that faith which is built upon Christ, who is the alone and proper sacrifice for sin."

9. Then she discoursed of the nature of faith, and desired that the 11th of the Hebrews should be read unto her: at the reading of which she cried out, "O what a steadfast faith was Abraham's, which made him willing to offer

up his own and only son! Faith is indeed the substance of things hoped for, the evidence of things not seen."

10. Her father and mother, seeing her, burst into tears; upon which she pleaded with them to be patient under the hand of God. "O," said she, "why do you weep over me, seeing you have no reason to question: but, if the Lord takes me, it shall be well with me to all eternity? You ought to be well satisfied, seeing it is said, 'God is in heaven, and doth whatever pleaseth him.' And do you not pray every day that the will of God may be done upon earth as it is in heaven? Now, father, this is God's will, that I should lie upon this sick bed, and die of this disease; shall we not be content when our prayers are answered? I will, as long as I live, pray that God's will be done, not mine."

11. "Doth not," said she, "the pestilence come from God? Why else doth the Scripture say, Shall there be evil in the city which I have not sent? Does it come from the air? And is not the Lord the Creator and Ruler of the air? Or if they say it comes from the earth, hath not he the same power and influence upon that too? What talk they of a ship that came from Africa? Have you not heard long ago, 'I will bring a sword upon you, and avenge the quarrel of my covenant, and when you are assembled in the cities, then I will bring the pestilence into the midst of you?'"

12. After this, having taken a little rest, she said, "Whether in death or life, a believer is Christ's, who hath redeemed us by his own precious blood from the power of the devil; then, whether I live or die, I am the Lord's. O why do you afflict yourselves thus? But what shall I say? With weeping I came into the world, and with weeping I must go out again. O my dear parents, better is the day of my death than the day of my birth."

13. She then desired her father to pray with her, and to request of the Lord that she might have a quiet passage into another world.

14. Her father, observing her to grow very weak, said, "I perceive, child, thou art very weak." "It is true, sir," said she, "I feel my weakness increasing, and I see your sorrow increasing too, which is a part of my affliction. Be content, I pray you, it is the Lord who does it; and let you and I say with David, 'Let us fall into the Lord's hand, for his mercies are great.'"

15. She laid a great charge upon her parents not to grieve for her after her death, urging that of David: while the child was sick he fasted and wept: but when it died he washed his face, and sat up, and ate, and said, "Can I bring him back from death? I shall go to him, but he shall not return to me."

16. Being very feeble, she said, "O that I might quietly sleep in the bosom of Jesus! and that till then he would strengthen me! O that he would take

me in his arms, as he did those little ones, where he said, 'Suffer little children to come unto me, for of such is the kingdom of heaven: and he took them in his arms, and he laid his hands on them, and blessed them,' I lie here as a child: O Lord, I am thy child, receive me into thy gracious arms. O Lord, grace! grace! and not justice! For if thou shouldst enter into judgment with me, I cannot stand: yea, none living would be just in thy sight."

17. Then she said, "O what is the life of man! The days of man upon earth are as grass, and as the flower of the field, so he flourishes: the wind passeth over it, and it is gone, and his place knows him no more."

18. She added, "My life shall not continue long. I feel much weakness: O Lord, look upon me graciously, have pity upon my weak distressed heart. I am oppressed, undertake for me, that I may stand fast and overcome."

19. She was very frequent in spiritual ejaculations, and it was no small comfort to her that the Lord Christ prayed for her, and promised to send his Spirit to comfort her. "It is said," continued she, "'I will pray the Father, and he shall give you another Comforter.' O let him not leave me! O Lord, stay with me till my battle and work is finished!"

20. Soon after, she said, "None but Christ; without thee I can do nothing! Christ is the true vine! O let me be a branch of that vine! What poor worms are we! O dear father, how lame and halting do we go on in the ways of God and salvation! We know but in part, but when that which is perfect is come, then that which is imperfect shall be done away. O that I had attained to that now! But what are we ourselves? Not only weakness and nothingness, but wickedness: for the thoughts and imaginations of a man's heart are only evil, and that continually. We are by nature children of wrath, and are conceived in sin, and born in unrighteousness! O this wretched and vile thing, sin! But thanks be to God, who hath redeemed me from it. O Lord, take me to thyself. Behold, dear mother, he has prepared a place for me."

21. "Yea, my dear child," said her mother, "He shall strengthen you with his Holy Spirit until he hath fitted and prepared you fully for that place which he hath provided for you."

22. "Yea, mother," replied she, "it is said in the 84th Psalm, 'How lovely are thy tabernacles, O Lord of hosts! My soul doth thirst and long for the courts of the Lord: one day in thy courts is better than a thousand: yea, I had rather be a door-keeper in the house of my God than dwell in the tents of the wicked.' Read that psalm, dear mother, wherewith we may comfort each other. As for me, I am more and more spent, and draw near my last hour."

23. Then she quoted Job's words, "I know that my Redeemer liveth, and that he shall stand at the latter day upon the earth: and though, after my skin, worms destroy this body, yet in my flesh shall I see God."

24. Then she said, "'Marvel not at this, for the hour is coming in which all that are in their graves shall hear his voice, and come forth; those that have done good unto the resurrection of life.' See, father, I shall rise in that day, and then I shall behold my Redeemer: then will he say, 'Come, ye blessed of my Father, inherit the kingdom prepared for you from the beginning of the world.' Behold, now I live, yet not I, but Christ liveth in me, and the life that I now live in the flesh, is by faith of the Son of God, who loved me, and gave himself for me. I am saved, and that not of myself, it is the gift of God; not of works, lest any man should boast."

25. "My dear parents, now we must part, my speech fails me: pray to the Lord for a quiet close to my combat." Her parents replied, "Ah, dear child! how sad is that to us, that we must part?" She answered, "I go to heaven, and there we shall find one another again: I go to Jesus Christ."

26. Then she comforted herself to think of her precious brother and sister. "I go to my brother Jacob, who did so much cry and call upon God to the last moment of his breath: and to my little sister, who was but three years old when she died: who, when we asked her whether she would die? answered, 'Yes, if it be the Lord's will.' I will go to my little brother, if it be the Lord's will, or I will stay with my mother, if it be his will. But I know that I shall die and go to heaven."

27. After this, her spirit was refreshed with a sense of the pardon of her sins, which made her to cry out, "Behold, God hath washed away my sins, O how I do long to die! The Lord is my shepherd: although I pass through the valley of the shadow of death, I will not fear, for thou art with me: shall I not suffer, seeing my glorious Redeemer was pleased to suffer so much for me? O how was he mocked and crowned with thorns, that he might purchase a crown of righteousness for us! Must I not exalt and bless him while I have a being, who hath bought me even with his blood! Behold the Lamb of God, that taketh away the sins of the world! That Lamb is Jesus Christ, who hath satisfied for my sins.

28. "My end is now very near; now I shall put on the white raiment, and be clothed before the Lamb, that spotless Lamb, and with his spotless righteousness. Now are the angels making ready to carry my soul before the throne of God. 'These are they who have come out of great tribulation, who have washed their robes, and made them white in the blood of the Lamb.'" She spoke this with a dying voice, but full of spirit and of the power of faith.

29. Her lively assurance she farther uttered in the words of the apostle, "We know that if this earthly house of our tabernacle be dissolved, we have a building of God, which is eternal in the heavens; for in this we sigh for our house which is in heaven; that we may be clothed therewith."

30. "There, father, you see that my body is this tabernacle, which now shall be broken down; my soul shall now part from it, and shall be taken up into paradise, into that heavenly Jerusalem. There shall I dwell and go no more out, but sit and sing, Holy, holy, is the Lord God of hosts, the Lord of Sabaoth!" Her last words were these: "O Lord God, into thy hands I commit my spirit: O Lord, be gracious, be merciful to me a poor sinner."

She died the first of September, 1664, between seven and eight in the evening; in the fourteenth year of her age.

THE MERCHANT'S SON.

JOHN HARVEY was born in London, in the year 1654: his father was a Dutch merchant: he was piously educated under his mother, and soon began to hear Divine things with delight.

2. The first thing observable in him was, that when he was two years and eight months old, he could speak as well as other children do usually at five years old.

3. His parents, judging that he was then too young to send to school, let him have his liberty to play about their yard, but instead of playing, he found out a school of his own accord near home, and went to the schoolmistress, and entreated her to teach him to read; and so he went some time to school without the knowledge of his parents, and made a very strange progress in his learning, and was able to read distinctly before most children knew their letters.

4. He was wont to ask many serious and weighty questions about matters which concerned his soul and eternity.

5. His mother being greatly troubled upon the death of one of his uncles, this child came to his mother and said, "Mother, though my uncle be dead, do not the Scriptures say he must rise again? Yes, and I must die, and so must every body, and it will not be long before Christ will come to judge the world, and then we shall see one another again: I pray mother, do not weep so much." He was not then quite five years old: by which her sorrow for her brother was turned into admiration, and she was made to sit silent and quiet under that trying providence.

6. After this his parents removed to Aberdeen, and settled their child under a schoolmaster there, whose custom was upon the Lord's day in the morning, to examine his scholars concerning the sermons they had heard the former Lord's day, and to add some other questions, which might try the understanding and knowledge of his scholars. The question that was once proposed to his form was, whether Christ had a mother? None of the scholars could answer it, till it came to John Harvey, who, being asked whether Christ had a mother? answered, "No; as he was God he could not have a mother; but as he was man he had." This was before he was six years old.

7. One day, seeing one of his near relations come into his father's house distempered with drink, he went to him, and wept over him, and besought him that he would not so offend God, and hazard his soul.

8. He was a conscientious observer of the Lord's day, spending all the time either in secret prayer, reading the Scriptures and good books, learning his catechism, or hearing the word of God. And he was not only careful in the performance of these duties himself, but was ready to put all that he knew upon a strict observation of the Lord's day.

9. He was very humble and modest, and hated any thing more than necessaries, either in clothes or diet.

10. When he perceived either his brother or sister pleased with their new clothes, he would reprove their folly; and when his reproof signified little, he would bewail their vanity.

11. Once he had a new suit brought from the tailor's, which, when he looked on, he found some ribands on the knees, at which he was grieved: asking his mother "whether these things would keep him warm?" "No, child," said his mother. "Why then," said he, "do you suffer them to be put there? You are mistaken if you think such things please me: and, I doubt some that are better than us may want the money that this cost you, to buy them bread."

12. At leisure times he was talking to his school fellows about the things of God, and the necessity of a holy life. That text he much spoke on to them, "The axe is laid to the root of the tree, and every tree that bringeth not forth good fruit is hewn down and cast into the fire."

13. After this his parents removed not far from London, where he continued till the year 1665. He was then sent to the Latin school, where he soon made a very considerable progress, and was greatly beloved of his master. The school was his beloved place, and learning his recreation.

14. He had a word to say to every one that he conversed with, to put them in mind of the worth of Christ and their souls; and their nearness to eternity: insomuch that good people took no small pleasure in his company.

15. He bewailed the miserable condition of the generality of mankind, (when he was about ten years old,) that they were utterly estranged from God. "Though they called him Father, he said, yet they were his children by creation, and not by any likeness they had to God, or any interest in him."

16. Thus he continued walking in the ways of God: in reading, praying, hearing the word of God, and spiritual intercourse; discovering thereby his serious thoughts of eternity, which seemed to swallow up all other thoughts; and he lived in a constant preparation for it, and looked more like one that was ripe for glory than an inhabitant of this lower world.17. When he was about eleven years and nine months old his mother's house was visited with the plague; his eldest sister was the first that was visited with

this distemper; and when they were praying for her, he would sob and weep bitterly.

18. As soon as he perceived his sister was dead, he said, "The will of the Lord be done2C blessed be the Lord! Dear mother, you must do as David did: after the child was dead he went and refreshed himself, and quietly submitted to the will of God."19. The rest of the family held well for some days, which time he spent in preparing for death. Meantime he wrote several meditations upon different subjects, particularly upon the excellence of Christ. He was never well but when he was more immediately engaged in the service of God.20. At the end of fourteen days he was taken sick, at which he seemed very cheerful; though his pains were great.21. His mother, looking upon his brother, shook her head: at which he asked if his brother was marked with the complaint? She answered, "Yea, child." He asked again whether he was marked? She answered nothing. "Well," says he, "I know I shall be marked: I pray let me have Mr. Baxter's book, that I may read a little more of eternity before I go into it." His mother told him he was not able to read. He said, "Then pray by me and for me."22. His mother asked him whether he was willing to die and leave her? He answered, "Yes. I am willing to leave you and go to my heavenly Father." She answered, "Child, if thou hadst but an assurance of God's love, I should not be so much troubled." He answered, "I am assured that my sins are forgiven, and that I shall go to heaven: for," said he, "here stood an angel by me, that told me I should quickly be in glory."23. At this his mother burst forth into tears. "O mother," said he, "did you but know what joy I feel you would not weep but rejoice. I tell you I am so full of comfort that I cannot tell you how I am: O mother, I shall presently have my head in my Father's bosom, and shall be there where the four and twenty elders cast down their crowns, and sing hallelujah, glory, and praise to him that sits upon the throne, and to the Lamb for ever!"24. Upon this his speech began to fail him, but his soul was still taken up with glory; and nothing now grieved him but the sorrow that he saw his mother to be in for his death; a little to divert her he asked, "What she had for supper?" But presently, in a kind of rapture he cried, "O what a sweet supper have I making ready for me in glory!"

25. But seeing all this did but increase his mother's grief, he asked her, "What she meant thus to offend God? Know you not that it is the hand of the Almighty? 'Humble yourself under the mighty hand of God:' lay yourself in the dust and kiss the rod, in token of your submission to the will of God." Upon which, raising himself a little, he gave a lowly bow, and spake no more! but went to rest in the bosom of Jesus.

PIOUS LITTLE PETER.

PETER MELVILLE, from the commencement of his illness, received much satisfaction from reading the Bible and other serious books; and after the first month or six weeks, was not known to read any other. The short history of Jesus Christ, by Mason, afforded him great satisfaction. In prayer he joined most heartily, and his eyes, while his friends were engaged in this exercise, were always raised toward heaven. During his painful illness, which lasted four months, he was remarkably patient, and much distressed at the idea of giving trouble. From these circumstances it was concluded that his mind was seriously disposed. Fourteen days, however, before his death, being much worse and unable to leave his bed, his anxious parents, desirous to know his real state, asked him if his mind was easy? At first he appeared inclined to evade the question; but the question being repeated he burst into tears and cried out, "I have been a very great sinner, I do not feel a love for my Saviour, nor see him with an eye of faith." Different texts of Scripture were mentioned which directed him to cast all his care on the Lord. These appeared to comfort him in a degree, and he then said, "What a charming place heaven is." It being observed that great advantages frequently resulted from a long illness, he expressed his sense of it by exclaiming, "What a dreadful place must I have gone to had I been cut off at once."

The next morning he was asked if he wished to converse with a minister? on his answering in the affirmative, the Rev. Mr. W. was requested to visit him; and was the instrument, in the hands of God, of composing his mind. The next day he requested that Watts' Psalms and Hymns, which he was very fond of reading, might be brought to him; and when his father came to his bedside he pointed to the 23d psalm, and asked if it was not a very sweet one?

On Saturday following he expressed a wish to have a Bible and prayer book purchased for him, in which, together with his hymn book, he wrote his name.

On Thursday, the 7th of April, being much worse, he was again asked if his mind was comfortable, to which he replied, "No; I am the greatest of sinners, and Satan tempts me to sin." Everything was said that could be thought of to compose him, and soon after he became more tranquil, and appeared delighted with the idea of heaven, requesting to have a description of that blessed place read to him. This had been done some time before, and had made a lasting impression on his mind. But when he made the request he added in a low voice, "I am afraid I shall never get there, because

I do not love my Saviour as I ought." Being asked again how he found his mind, he answered, "A little better; but I wish to love my Lord and Saviour; and I hope to be able to do it more and more."

On being reminded that it was Good Friday, he talked much of our Lord's great sufferings for his people; and while speaking of the blessed Lamb that had been crucified on that day, he desired the 25th hymn of the third book of Watts to be read to him.

"All mortal vanities, begone."

On the evening of this day he appeared to feel much of what had been said to him by the Rev. Mr. H., who had visited him frequently.

Saturday night was spent in great pain—he had but few intervals of ease. When he was told "such things were from the Lord," he replied, "The Lord is good, yes, the Lord is good to them who put their trust in him." When he expressed his gratitude to his weeping parents for their attention to him, and his mother had told him that it was the Lord who enabled them to do any thing for him, and mentioned his glorious Saviour as the blessed object of all his gratitude, he turned his thoughts to heaven and said, "Then I hope to love him now; and what rapture will it afford me to meet all my dear friends with him in glory." He spoke for some time on the subject with great energy; and on being told that he would fatigue himself, he replied, "It is not fatiguing, it is rapturous;" and particularly expressed a hope that not one of his family would be *wanting;* adding, "What a disappointment shall I feel if you are not there." He seemed much refreshed by this conversation, and went to sleep with a sweet smile on his countenance.

In the afternoon he was still more composed, and told his mother he would talk a little; when he again dwelt most sweetly on the goodness of the Lord to his soul, and the happiness of meeting his parents and friends in glory. In the night, being asked if he did not love the sinner's friend, he replied, "I wish to do it, and in heaven I shall do it more," adding, "No one ever loved him one part in a thousand so much as they ought to do." He frequently prayed for patience, being subject to great pain. Seeing his mother weep, he asked her why she cried. She replied, "That she could not help it." "I hope," said he, "the Lord will give you strength."

On the Monday, being again frequently asked if Jesus was precious, he at times nodded his head, and at others said, "I hope he is, and that he will be more so by and by." But soon after that he said, "I am a great sinner, and am afraid I shall be disappointed in all my hopes of heaven." But being exhorted to cast all his unbelieving thoughts away, and put his entire trust in his blessed Redeemer, whose arms were underneath him, he replied, "Then I am safe." Again he thanked his parents for their care of him, and when it was repeated that it was all the Lord's doing, "Then," said he, "you are the instruments, and what a blessed thing it is to have parents who guide and instruct us in the way;" and added, "O what will become of those children who idle about on the Sabbath day, who swear and steal. O shocking! shocking! O what a blessing to have good parents." On requesting to see his brothers, they came to him; and taking them by the hand, he asked them how they did. To his little brother Henry he said, "Be a good boy, do not run about with idle children, and tell Philip what I say, learn your catechism, also read your Bible." Perceiving that his eldest brother cried, he said, "Why is John weeping? Weep not for me, weep for yourselves." "What a blessed change," said a friend, "will it be, from such a sick bed as this to the joys of heaven!" to which he added, "To be in the arms of my Redeemer, to see him face to face, and behold his glories in heaven: O how admirable! O what are the glories of an earthly kingdom when compared to this: but as the drop of a bucket to the ocean; yea, no mortal can describe the joys of heaven." When he again sweetly dwelt on the happiness of meeting all his friends there, "Where," said he, "we shall meet to part no more for ever; and there shall be no more death;" which he twice repeated. In the night he was much buffeted by Satan. About four o'clock in the morning, he appeared to be dying, and in a low voice, said, "May you all keep the commandments, and love God evermore. Weep not for me, I am not worth weeping for." Being in an agony of pain he was directed to the source of all good. Soon after he appeared easier, and said, "Truly the heart is willing, but the flesh is weak, and if the heart is willing, never mind the voice." Being reminded of the joy he would feel at hearing his Lord say, "Well done, good and faithful servant, enter thou into the joy of thy Lord;" he exclaimed, "Amen, so be it," and spoke no more. "Great are the troubles of the righteous, but the Lord delivereth out of them all," was the last text repeated to him, to which he nodded his head, and then calmly fell asleep in Jesus, aged twelve years and three months.

Farewell, dear babe, with all thy sacred store,
In triumph landed on the heavenly shore;
Sure nature form'd thee in her softest mould,
And grace, from nature's dross, refund the gold.

THE DUTIFUL DAUGHTER.

ELIZABETH W. ORCHARD was born March 6, 1795, at Melksham, in Wiltshire; and from an early age was very dutiful to her parents, and much attached to her school and books. In 1802 her father removed from Newport, in the Isle of Wight, to Bath; where he and his family attended the Rev. Mr. J.'s chapel. Soon after their arrival at Bath, Elizabeth and William her brother were admitted into the Sunday school belonging to Argyle chapel; from the time of Elizabeth's admittance, she seemed to read her books with understanding and profit; and during the week, it was always her study to get her task by heart against the returning Sabbath. Her partiality for her teachers was great: especially for Miss S., whom, when she was taken ill, she longed to see. The tickets that were given to her in the school, as tokens for good, she valued much; and expressed a wish to return them, that she might obtain a hymn book, the reward she was entitled to. A shilling that was given to her by the committee at Christmas, for learning her book, with one that she had borrowed of her brother, she laid out in the purchase of a Testament; which she preserved with great care till her departure.

During her illness, Elizabeth often reproved her brother and sister, saying, "If you are not better you will certainly go to a place of misery." On every occasion she discovered a great love to prayer; and when by weakness she was prevented from going to chapel, she learned her tasks; and what she did learn and hear, was, by a Divine blessing, deeply impressed on her mind.

For the last five weeks before her death, she was not in the least terrified at her approaching dissolution; but conversed with pleasure on her departure. Her father asked her one day, when in great pain, whether she loved the Lord and Saviour Jesus Christ? to which she answered, "Yes, I do, and I shall soon be with him in glory." Mr. B., one of the teachers of the school, called to see her; and after conversing with her some time, asked her, "If she should like to go to heaven?" to which she answered, "Yes."

On April the 24th, when in great pain, on viewing her hands, she said, "O father! the blood ran from the hands of Jesus Christ when he was nailed to the cross, and that was done by wicked men, but I shall go and see him in heaven." At another time, when her parents, talking of the sufferings of Christ, said that he died to save good children, and would take them to sit with him on his throne for ever, and would give them crowns of glory. To which she answered, "It seems, father, as if I could see him." On the same day she said, "I do hope when my body dies, that God will receive my soul to heaven." After this she related to her parents the account of the rich man in the Gospel; observing that he was tormented in hell, and could not so much as obtain a drop of water to cool his burning tongue, while poor Lazarus was carried to Abraham's bosom, where he was crowned with happiness.

She was visited by her much beloved teacher Miss S., whom she had long wished to see; and to whom, with the rest of the teachers of the school, her parents say they shall be always thankful for the good instruction they gave their dear departed child; and hope that the committee and teachers of the school at Argyle chapel, and of every other similar school, will be encouraged by this instance of the good effects of religious advice in a child only nine years old, to go forward in their endeavours to bring young sinners to Christ. She was much struck with a passage of Scripture in Revelation, that Mr. J. preached from: "They shall be clothed in white." "O," said Elizabeth, "I expect to be clothed in white too." And as her mother was sitting by her bedside reading, she said, "If God will let me, I will keep places for you who may be left behind." Her brother she advised not to play so much, but to be a good boy, mind his book and school, and pray to God to make him truly religious; or he would go to a place of misery after death. Being told that she was very ill, she replied, "I must bear it with patience:" though, in fact, she longed to be gone. When she was very weak, and death stared in her face, her parents carried her from one room to another; but in no place could she find ease. She, however, contemplated with satisfaction the day when she should eat of the tree of life that grows in the midst of the paradise of God; "There," said Elizabeth, "I shall never thirst, nor never sin, but behold the Lamb, who will lead me to fountains of living water." After lying one day in a doze, she opened her eyes and said, "Mother, I have seen an angel." Her mother asked her where? She pointed to the place where she dreamed that she saw him. And, being asked if she should like to go with him, she answered, "Yes."

"There I shall see his face,
And never, never sin;
There from the rivers of his grace
Drink endless pleasures in."

Her parents now hung mournfully around her bed, and concluded that the Lord was going to release her. They saw clearly that she could not survive long. Being raised up on the following Sabbath in bed, by pillows, and seeing the children in the street at play, she observed to them about her how improper it was that they should profane the Sabbath, and that they ought to be at chapel, and that God would be very angry with them. Her father had some time before carried her out for the benefit of the air, daily. And being out with her the Sabbath before her departure, she pressed him to carry her to chapel; which he did, but was soon obliged to return with her, when she exclaimed, "Farewell, chapel; farewell, Mr. J.; farewell, my beloved teachers; farewell, my dear schoolfellows;" and soon after she said, "Farewell, brother and sister; farewell, father and mother. I charge you all to meet me in heaven, that we may spend an eternity of happiness together there." And on the 27th of May, 1804, after a few struggles, the feeble springs of life stood still, and her happy spirit took its flight to the paradise of God.